Tell Me Why

WHY?

It Snows

Tamra B. Orr

Published in the United States of America by Cherry Lake Publishing
Ann Arbor, Michigan
www.cherrylakepublishing.com

Content Adviser: Jack Williams, science writer specializing in weather
Reading Adviser: Marla Conn, ReadAbility, Inc.

Photo Credits: © Pete Pahham/Shutterstock Images, cover, 1, 11; © Dalton Dingelstad/Shutterstock Images,
cover, 1, 19; © Digital Media Pro/Shutterstock Images, cover, 1, 15; © Nancy Bauer/Shutterstock Images,
cover; © Maria Uspenskaya/Shutterstock Images, cover; © Terric Delayn/Shutterstock Images, cover;
© JaySi/Shutterstock Images, 5; © V. J. Matthew/Shutterstock Images, 7; © Kim Steele/Thinkstock, 9;
© Sergei Butorin/Shutterstock Images, 11; © Jamie Hooper/Shutterstock Images, 13; © Kichigin/
Shutterstock Images, 15; © Mike Watson Images/Thinkstock, 17; © Galyna Andrushko/Shutterstock
Images, 19; © JeremyTaylor/Shutterstock Images, 21

Library of Congress Cataloging-in-Publication Data

Orr, Tamra.
  It snows / Tamra B. Orr.
    pages cm -- (Tell me why)
  Includes index.
  Summary: "Young children are naturally curious about the world around
them. It Snows offers answers to their most compelling questions about
winter weather. Age-appropriate explanations and appealing photos encourage
readers to continue their quest for knowledge. Additional text features and
search tools, including a glossary and an index, help students locate
information and learn new words"—Provided by publisher.
  Audience: 6-10.
  Audience: K-Grade 3.
  ISBN 978-1-63188-998-1 (hardcover) -- ISBN 978-1-63362-076-6 (pdf) -- ISBN
978-1-63362-037-7 (pbk.) -- ISBN 978-1-63362-115-2 (ebook)
1. Snow--Juvenile literature. 2. Blizzards--Juvenile literature. 3. Weather forecasting--Juvenile
literature. I. Title. II. Series: Tell me why (Cherry Lake Publishing)

QC926.37.O77 2015
551.57'84--dc23

                    2014031832

Cherry Lake Publishing would like to acknowledge the work of The Partnership for 21st Century Skills.
Please visit *www.p21.org* for more information.

Printed in the United States of America.
Corporate Graphics

Table of Contents

Watching the Sky

Taylor looked out the front window and stared up at the afternoon sky. "Taylor, what are you looking for?" asked his mother.

"Watching for **snowflakes**," he replied. "We might get a snowstorm tonight. I want to see it start."

"Let's watch a weather report and see what the **forecast** is. We can find out if it's going to snow."

As long as you wear warm clothes, playing in the snow can be fun.

"It's winter, and it's cold. So why wouldn't it snow?" asked Taylor.

"The chilly temperatures are only part of the equation," she said. "You need one other factor. Can you guess what it is?"

"Water! You have to have water," Taylor guessed.

Taylor's mother nodded and turned on the television. "Exactly! Come on. Let's find out if a snow day is in your future."

It may not be safe for school buses to travel after a snowstorm.
That is a reason to close school.

A Weather Advisory

"Jefferson County is under a winter weather **advisory** until 6 p.m." The man talking was the **meteorologist** for the local news station.

"What does that mean?" asked Taylor.

"Winter storms have codes," explained Mom. "An advisory means there is a chance of a storm."

Winter storms are huge swirls made of cold, dry air from the north, and warm, **moist** air from the south. The cold air shoves under the lighter warm air, pushing it up. This turns

Meteorologists study weather and share the forecast.

the moisture in the warm air into clouds. These clouds can produce snow for some places, rain for others. Sometimes the storm arrives with rain, which then turns to snow.

An hour later, Mom stuck her head in Taylor's bedroom. "You got your wish! The weather report just said we are in for a **blizzard**. I think I just spotted the first flakes."

"Snow day!" Taylor cheered.

Clearing roads for safe driving takes time and equipment.

Snowstorm Science

Long before the first snowflake floats to the ground, it is being created up in the air. **Water vapor** inside the clouds meets freezing temperatures and turns into ice.

These tiny **snow crystals** are sticky. As many as 200 of them can clump together and form a snowflake. Then it drops out of the cloud and falls to the ground.

"Wow, look at those flakes!" exclaimed Taylor, pointing outside. "Is it really true that no two are alike?"

If you look closely, you can see the differences in snowflakes.

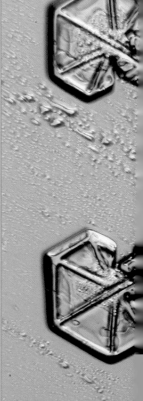

"Yes," replied Mom. "They are like people. Each one is a little bit different."

"It's confirmed. We have a blizzard," said the newscaster. "Stay inside and safe."

Not all winter storms are blizzards. A blizzard combines snow with strong winds. It lasts for at least 3 hours. Blowing snow can create **whiteouts** and make driving dangerous.

Look closely at this photo of a snowflake. Do you see the six sides?

All snow crystals have six sides.

When Snow Gets Scary

"Do you think Grandma Maryann is getting lots of snow, too?" asked Taylor.

Mom laughed. "No, she's nice and warm in Southern California. The mountains in California get a lot of snow, but not where Grandma lives."

It hardly ever snows in the southern parts of the United States.

"Our mailbox is buried!" said Taylor the next morning. "Are we in danger of an **avalanche**?"

"No. Those only happen on mountains," said his mother.

Avalanches happen after a lot of new snow has fallen on top of older snow.

Have you heard of a nor'easter or thunder snow? These are types of winter storms. Go online with an adult to find out more about each.

Avalanches happen on mountain slopes.

Gravity pushes down on the snow at the top of a steep slope. A sudden, loud noise or temperature change can send tons of snow sliding down the mountain. It can travel at speeds of 100 to 300 mph (161 to 483 kph). The avalanche can knock down trees, buildings, and people.

"Whew!" said Taylor. "In that case, I'm going out to play in the snow."

Warning signs are posted near places where an avalanche could happen.

Think About It

Let's say you found out your city is going to have a blizzard. What are some things you and your family can do to prepare for it?

Do you live near a lake or body of water? Have you ever heard of "lake-effect snow"? Go online with an adult or visit your local library to find out what it means.

Glossary

advisory (ad-VYE-zuh-ree) a bulletin that warns the public of a possible danger

avalanche (AV-uh-lanch) a large mass of snow sliding down a mountainside

blizzard (BLIZ-erd) a storm combining snow and wind and lasting for hours

forecast (FOHR-kahst) a prediction

meteorologist (mee-tee-uh-RAH-luh-jist) an expert who studies weather

moist (MOIST) slightly wet

snow crystals (SNOH KRIS-tuhlz) small, six-sided pieces of the solid form of water (ice)

snowflakes (SNOH-fleykz) collections of snow crystals that are stuck together

water vapor (WAW-ter VEY-per) the invisible gas form of water

whiteouts (WHYT-outs) conditions of limited visibility caused by heavily falling and blowing snow

Find Out More

Books:

Cassino, Mark. *The Story of Snow: The Science of Winter's Wonder*. San Francisco: Chronicle Books, 2009.

Danks, Fiona. *The Wild Weather Book: Loads of Things to Do Outdoors in Rain, Wind, and Snow*. London: Frances Lincoln Books, 2013.

Libbrecht, Kenneth. *The Secret Life of a Snowflake: An Up-Close Look at the Art and Science of Snowflakes*. London: Voyageur Press, 2009.

Web Sites:

Live Science—The 9 Snowiest Places on Earth
www.livescience.com/30097-the-snowiest-places-on-earth.html
See photos and read facts about places that often face extreme weather.

USA Today—Answers Archive: Winter, Snow, Ice
http://usatoday30.usatoday.com/weather/resources/askjack/wasnow.htm
Find answers to some of the most popular questions about winter weather.

Index

About the Author

Tamra Orr is a full-time author living in the Pacific Northwest. Originally from Indiana, she was used to snowstorms. Now she lives where it rarely snows in the city, but snow blankets the mountains all around her. She is a mom to four, a graduate of Ball State University, and the author of more than 350 books for readers of all ages.